WALLACE TRIPP'S

Virgin on the Ridiculous

WALLACE TRIPP'S

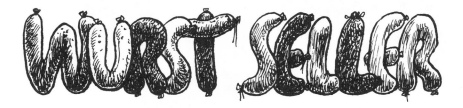
WURST SELLER

AS KEEN A WEEN AS
EVER I'VE SEEN, BUT
NOW I'M GOING GREEN.

Sparhawk Books Inc
Jaffrey, New Hampshire

for Marcy

Tripp, Wallace.
   Wallace Tripp's Wurst Seller.

   1. American wit and humor. I. Title. II. Title:
Wurst Seller.
PN6162.T68 1981   818'.5402   81-4781
ISBN 0-9605776-1-0   AACR2

ISBN 0-9605776-0-2

Printed in the United States of America

Li'l Orphan Spruntly

YA SHOONTA ATE MY DOG UP LIKE THAT, YA BIG LUMMOX. OH WELL, NOT NICE HOLDIN' A GRUDGE, IS IT? YA KNOW, COME TO THINK OF IT, WITH A PAL LIKE YOU I WOULDN'T HAVE TO RELY ON MY BRAINS AND CHARM TO OUTWIT ALL THOSE SNOBS, KIDNAPPERS, COMMIES, CONMEN, LIBERALS, AGENTS PROVOCATEURS, SADISTS, MISERS, AND ED CEDDERA. NO SIREE, YOU COULD JUST TEAR THE BASKETS TO BITS. SAY, YOON ME GONNA RULE THE GOL-DANG WORLD.

ORF.

Mozart's Lost Trio: "The Buccina"

Dehydrated frog

Same frog, too
much water added

Squeaking
wheel which
got the grease

I STINK,
THEREFORE
I AM.

Girl who is
a perfect
ten

Careless hedgehog
after roll in
the apples

Apostle
firing off
epistle

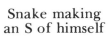

Snake making
an S of himself

Otter gargling
to check his
neck for leaks

William
the Conker

British variant.

Fred was a
leg man

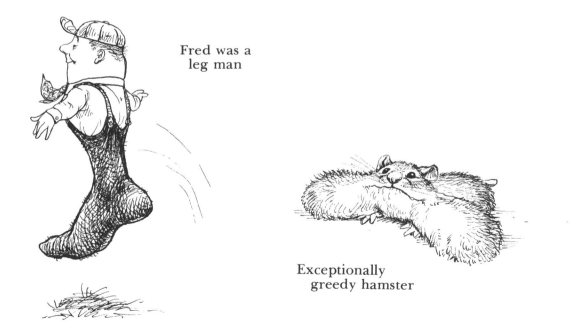

Exceptionally
greedy hamster

Choir Practice

hair center part
true eyes
whiskers
flat navel

True Nym

no hair part
green eyes
sideburns
recessed navel

Pseudo Nym

ocelli tend to form broken
longitudinal lines over shoulder
1 row postrostrala
dorsal scales 93 or more
45 or more scales between interparietal
and rear of thigh
complete
supraorbital
semicircles

ticklish feet

Genuine Modo

gular fold present
2 rows postrostrala
dorsal scales 92 or fewer
42 or fewer scales interparietal
to rear of thigh.
incomplete
supraorbital
semicircles

ticklish belly

Quasi Modo

THINK FAST,
MR. MODO

Pie a la Modo

Quasi Quasimodo

Queasy Quasimodo

Gnome de Plume

The Sack of Rome

Jack the
Ripper

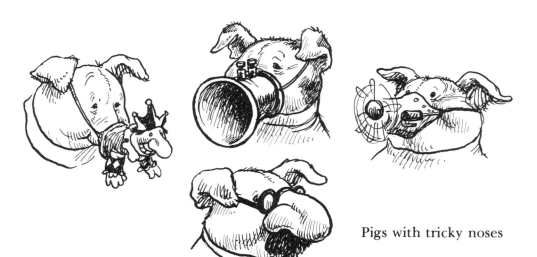

Pigs with tricky noses

Primavera – 1942

Dante in the Lumbar Region

A word to the wide is sufficient

Poet with well-furnished mind

Tennis player with
vicious backhand

In subtle but unmistakable ways
the dog began to insinuate himself
into Ted's life

Close encounters of the fourth kind

The Mythical King Alexander Borne Aloft by Griffins

ON SAFARI IN DEEPEST AUSTRIA, LADY SNEAZEGROIN GIVES BIRTH TO A SON. SAVAGE ABBERATIONES WIPE OUT THE EXPEDITION, BUT THE INFANT IS RESCUED BY GREAT GREY KANGAROOS AND RAISED BY BONGA, THEIR MIGHTY QUEEN, WHO GRIEVES AT THE LOSS OF HER ONLY SON. LEARNING THE ANCIENT LORE AND WISDOM OF THIS MAGNIFICENT RACE, THE FOUNDLING BECOMES...

KANGA BOY
LORD OF THE BUSH AND LEAPER SUPREME

HE'S ABOVE AIR FRIDGE

JOEY TO THE WORLD

SPA FON

LAST WEEK KANGA BOY, WITH THE AID OF HIS FAITHFUL COMPANION PHASCO AND THE GREAT GREY EMINENCES, DEFEATED THE FOUR HORSEMEN OF THE ARCHIPELAGO. NOW THEY MEET THE DEADLIEST FOES OF ALL — THE WOMBATS OF DEATH.

ATTACKING WITH HIS LASER WOMBAT-COMBAT DOOMERANGS KANGA BOY SHOUTS THE WAR CRY OF THE GREAT GREYS...

WOGGA!

HOLY EUCALYPTUS!

DINKUM BUNDOLO, MITE

SPLUT!
WHUNG!
SNOCK!
LAPOOSH
SHUNK
COBBER
PLOOD!
BOK!
STREWTH!
CHONG!

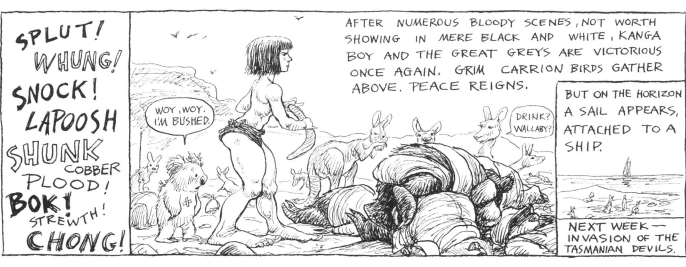

WOY, WOY. I'M BUSHED.

DRINK? WALLABY?

AFTER NUMEROUS BLOODY SCENES, NOT WORTH SHOWING IN MERE BLACK AND WHITE, KANGA BOY AND THE GREAT GREYS ARE VICTORIOUS ONCE AGAIN. GRIM CARRION BIRDS GATHER ABOVE. PEACE REIGNS.

BUT ON THE HORIZON A SAIL APPEARS, ATTACHED TO A SHIP.

NEXT WEEK — INVASION OF THE TASMANIAN DEVILS.

BOY. OH BOY OH BOY. BOYOBOYOBOY. WADDA DAY. BOYOHBOY. BOY.

The wolf who cried "Boy."

Missing Person's Bureau

← MISSING LYNX

HEY, WHAT'S THE SCOOP, BOOPY-DOOP? HEY, HEY. YING-A-DING, YOU PRIDDY THING. WOO, WOOO, WOOOO.

Despite his classic good looks and mellifluous voice, Harry seemed to make little headway with women.

The Winds Swirled and a Mighty Music
Sounded in his Ears and through his Tears
there Shimmered and Gleamed the Russet Lady
in Honeyed Tones Murmuring Over and Again
the Word of All Magic, All Power . . .

Eye Doctor

Brain Surgeon

Plastic Surgeon

Tree Surgeon

Podiatrist in toe truck
pursuing arch enemy

Navel Surgeon

A Dog's Life

by NEDDY DINGO

YOU A DOG?

YEAH AND VERILY. SURE. WOOF. WOOF.

THE TRUTH NOW!

IN TROOT, I HAVE A PEDIGREASE FROM TWENNY GERMINATIONS BACKWARD, O BACKWARD, TIME IN HIM FLIGHT. I HAVE A WAGON IN MY TAIL AND A ANTINK OLD BONE COLLECTION WORTH PEARL BEYOND PRIDES.

OH, COULD I BUT BE CERTAIN. I AM SURE OF NOTHING BUT THE HOLINESS OF THE HEART'S AFFECTIONS AND THE TRUTH OF THE IMAGINATION.

CHEESE. MAYBE I BEDDA HAVE ANNUDA LOOK.

PROB'LY I'M A DOG.

THE LAWS OF PROBABILITY: SO TRUE IN GENERAL; SO FALLACIOUS IN PARTICULAR.

AND YET... AND YET, A MOMENT'S INSIGHT IS SOMETIMES WORTH A LIFE'S EXPERIENCE. I BEGIN TO SENSE, TO FEEL, YES, TO **KNOW** YOU ARE A DOG. OH, CLEANSE MY DOUBTING SPIRIT, GRATEFUL BALM OF CERTITUDE FROM ON HIGH.

WOW! I HOPE I'M NOT A HIPPOPOST-OMOCKS. I CAN'T SWIM.

OH, DOG! THE CRUEL NIGHT OF MY DOUBT HAS PASSED AND YOU HAVE BECOME TO ME DOG IN TRUTH, DOG TANGIBLE, DOG SUBSTANTIVE, AND DOGGINESS ITSELF.

HEY, NEAT! DEN IT'S O.K. FOR ME TO SCOFF DIS BONE.

DOG, NOW IT CAN BE TOLD. THERE IS A NOVEL IN ME, SCREAMING FOR RELEASE.

MUM.

I HAVE A TALE TO TELL! BUT WILL THE BENUMBED AND SOMNOLENT WORLD, MIRED IN THE BASE AND MINDLESS ROUTINE OF LIFE, HAVE EARS TO LISTEN?

PARDON?

HMMPH! YOU, SIR, ARE A PHILISTINE.

A LOT HE KNOWS. I'M WELSH.

Freud Egg

Oedipus complex

Oedipus simple

A flash in the pan

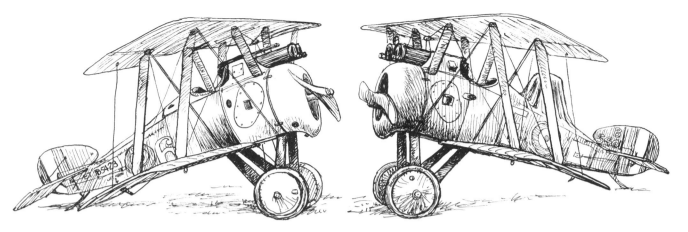

Sopwith Camel (Dromedary)   Sopwith Camel (Bactrian)

Silver hares around the temples

Silver hares among the gold

Bavarian Radio Orchestra

The Sentinels

Jim's back.   Jim's back again.   Oh no! Jim's back a third time.   Thank goodness. Jim's left.

Hark! Tis the mewling sun, all anxious fired
To bait the breath of bilious day betimes.
And yet, so fair is she, the very sun
Doth in his nether galligaskins run
And leap, all brass-infested 'bout the brain;
And weighty words saith he, fall'n down like stones:
"Thou speak'st with art, young maid, but art thou true
And truly to the truth betrothed, or say,
Married up; marry, with a golden ring
Made gilt, with guilt and wrong disbarred, by troth,
So ring thy words more gold, well-goaled and round,
Wrung from truth, ringing true, like gold unmarred?"
But, strained amain, his brain doth burst apart.
Thus ends our tale quite near its grievous start.

ABOUT TO LOSE
HIS POETIC LICENSE

Fred knitting his brow

OH DARN.
OH KNITS.
SEW CREWEL.

Fred coming unraveled

Girl unsuited for her work

A Rose-red Sidney —
half as old as Tom

Venus Fly Trap

Flying Dutchman Over chewer

LITTLE BUNNY WUFFY and TEE WEE
by Mitzy

C'MON, TEE WEE, IT'S A WUVLEY DAY. LET'S GO OUT AND WOMP AND PWAY.

PLAY?

DON'T LOOK SO GLUM, MITHTA CWOW! THE SUN IS IN THE SKY, YOU KNOW!

NO?

POOR OL' CWOW. HE LOOKED SO SAD. I GUESS WE CHANGED HIS DAY TO GLAD

GLAD?

DO NOT CWY, DEAR MRS. MOUSE, BECAUSE THE WATS DESTWOYED YOUR HOUSE...

HOUSE?

...AND ATE YOUR BABIES OFF THE FLOOR. IN THIRTY DAYS YOU'LL HAVE SOME MORE.

MORE?

I THINK WE CHEERED THAT SAD MOUSEWIFE. YOU HAVE TO SEE THE FUN IN WIFE.

LIFE?

BOO! I SCARED YOU, MR. TOAD! OH, HE'S FAINTED ON THE WOAD.

ROAD?

NO, NOT FAINTED. HE'S CWOAKED, I THINK. BUT HE WAS OLD AND WEAK FWOM DWINK.

DRINK?

I ATE HIM NOT FOR NEED OF FOOD. I DID IT FOR THE COMMON GOOD.

GOOD!

Rabbit speaking in
broken Italian

The late Letitia Shrew
attacking sleeping tiger

"They're almost ready, General."

Billy Jim Goatsprig,
the notorious cat poisoner

Darius the Meaty

I THINK,
THEREFORE
I YAM.

Atilla the Bun

Orator in sudden burst of elephants

Man waxing elephant

Alexander the Mastodon

"... A GLORIOUS PHANTOM MAY BURST TO ILLUMINE OUR TEMPESTUOUS DAY." REALLY, PERCY B.!

Nelly Kelly with her belly full of Botticelli Jelly, reading Shelley

Chaste maidens

Mark Twain answers his critics

Beauty in the eye of the beholder

When knighthood was in flour

Weighed in the
balance and
found wincing

GERONIMO!

VICTORIO!

COCHISE!

The Bugler's Funeral

THE LESSER OF TWO WEEVILS

Time flies like an arrow.
Fruit flies like a banana.

THAT WAS NO LADYBUG.
THAT WAS MY WIFE.

WANNA COME
UP AND SEE
MY ITCHINGS?

Too many
moths to feed.

WITH CALM, WITH RESOLUTION, HE
ABJURES ALL — BOTTLE, FRESH
DIAPER, SECONDS OF DUTCH APPLE,
AND WILLY CHOB CHOB HIS
STUFFED BEAR — KNOWING, AS
ONLY HE CAN KNOW, THAT...